Before the Sirens
A Teacher's Role in Leading Through School Emergencies

by
Kenneth Lacey
&
David Fraszka

Copyright © 2025 by First 5 Consulting Group Inc.

All rights reserved. No part of this book may be reproduced, stored in a retrieval system, or transmitted in any form or by any means — electronic, mechanical, photocopying, recording, or otherwise — without the prior written permission of the publisher, except for brief quotations used in reviews or educational settings.

ISBN: 979-8-9987920-0-7

Published by First 5 Consulting Group Inc.

For information, training inquiries, or bulk orders, please contact: kd@first5consulting.com

Cover design and interior layout by First 5 Consulting Group Inc.

Printed in the United States of America

Table of Contents

Part I: Foundations of School Safety
    Chapter 1: Why Teachers Are the Real First Responders 4
    Chapter 2: Understand the SHELL Protocols 8

Part II: Responding in Real Time
    Chapter 3: The Art of Calm- Communicating Under Pressure 19
    Chapter 4: Leading Students When the Alarm Sounds 24

Part III: Prevention and Awareness
    Chapter 5: Recognizing Red Flags – Behavior Before Crisis .. 32
    Chapter 6: De-escalation in the Classroom 41
    Chapter 7: When Police Arrive 48

Part IV: Resilience & Recovery
    Chapter 8: After the Emergency - Recovery Starts With You 54
    Chapter 9: Facing the Fear – Changing the Culture 62

Sources and Acknowledgments 69

Preface

At First 5 Consulting Group, we've spent years walking school hallways, meeting with educators, and guiding leaders through the complex—and often emotionally charged—work of keeping schools safe. Over time, one truth has become crystal clear:

Teachers are the real first responders.

Before the principal announces a lockdown... before emergency services arrive... before a threat can be fully assessed... it's the teacher at the front of the classroom who leads, shields, reassures, and protects. You are the anchor in the room when everything else feels uncertain.

This guide was written with *you* in mind.

We know your job is already full—lesson planning, parent communications, grading, classroom management—and the idea of "adding emergency response to your plate" can feel overwhelming. That's not what we're here to do. Instead, we've designed this guide to help you approach school safety with **clarity, confidence, and purpose.**

This book is not a policy manual or a compliance checklist. It won't try to answer every "what if" or replace your school's formal emergency plans. And it won't load you down with acronyms or technical jargon. **What it *will* do is get you thinking—really thinking—about how you respond in the first five minutes of a crisis.**

Because in those first five minutes, your mindset matters. Your voice matters. Your ability to stay calm, make decisions, and lead your students matters more than any written plan.

Throughout this book, we'll draw from real-world experience working with schools across New York and beyond. We'll walk through common safety protocols like SHELL, introduce practical classroom strategies, and share stories that highlight what *works*—and why it matters.

We wrote this to be short on theory and long on action. It's meant to be read in one sitting or used over time in small pieces. Our hope is that this book becomes part of your school's broader safety conversation—and maybe even something you discuss with your team during staff meetings or professional development sessions.

We believe deeply in the mission of education. And we believe that school safety isn't just the job of administrators or security staff—it's a shared responsibility. Not out of fear, but out of commitment. Not to scare, but to prepare.

Thank you for being the calm in the storm—for being ready to lead, and ready to shield.

Let's get started

Part I: Foundations of School Safety

Chapter 1

Why Teachers Are the Real First Responders

On December 14, 2012, a first-grade teacher named **Kaitlyn Roig** found herself facing the unthinkable.

She was in her classroom at Sandy Hook Elementary School when gunfire erupted just outside her door. There was no warning. No announcement. Just terror, chaos, and the split-second decision to act.

She didn't wait.
She didn't hesitate.
She didn't freeze.

Instead, Kaitlyn gathered her fifteen students and ushered them into a tiny, single-occupancy bathroom, locking the door behind them. She told them to climb on top of the toilet seats. She told them to be completely silent. And she told them—just in case it was the last thing they ever heard—that she loved them.

When a voice called from outside the door, claiming to be the police, she didn't open it. She trusted her gut. She stayed quiet. She waited.

Every one of her students survived.

Later, she would describe the moment not as one of heroism, but one of preparation. She had thought about what she might do. She had made a mental plan. And when the unimaginable happened, she was able to act—quickly, decisively, and without panic.

There was no emergency manual in her hands. No checklist. Just instinct, composure, and resolve.

That moment is why we say this:

Teachers are the real first responders.

The Purpose of This Manual

Emergency plans, security systems, and drills all play a critical role in school safety. But in the first few minutes of a crisis, it is often the teacher standing in the classroom who becomes the first—and sometimes only—person able to take protective action.

It's the teacher who locks the door.
The teacher who leads the evacuation.
The teacher who calms frightened children and manages the unknown until help arrives.

You may not wear a badge or carry a radio.
But in those first critical moments, **you are the leader your students need most.**

This book was created to honor that role—and to support you in it.
We're not here to scare you.
We're here to help you feel steady, informed, and capable—just like Kaitlyn Roig was in that bathroom.

The First 5 Minutes Matter

In our work with schools, we often use the phrase **"the first five."** It's a reference to those critical first five minutes of an emergency—

when everything is still unfolding, and you may not yet have instructions or outside help. In those moments, your mindset matters more than any title or training.

We've seen time and again how teacher presence—calm voices, clear direction, and steady leadership—sets the tone for student safety and survival. Whether the situation is a fire alarm, an intruder threat, a medical emergency, or even a natural disaster, students look to their teacher as the person who *knows what to do.*

That doesn't mean you need to be fearless. It means that you've prepared your classroom, practiced your protocols, and know your first move—even if the rest is unclear.

Your Role Is Bigger Than You Think

Many educators hesitate when they hear phrases like *school security* or *crisis response*. They think, "That's not my job—that's for the safety team." But in a school environment, safety is a **shared responsibility.** And in fact, it is teachers who most often notice when a student is in distress… who are first on scene when something goes wrong… and who can make the difference between order and chaos in those early moments.

This book is about helping you see that role clearly—and giving you practical, realistic ways to step into it with confidence.

You don't have to be perfect. You just have to be ready.

Prepared, Not Paranoid

One thing we want to make clear right away: our goal is not to make you fearful. We are not here to "what if" you into anxiety.

Instead, we want to help you build a **mindset of preparedness**—the kind that Kaitlyn Roig exemplified under impossible circumstances. Her story is not one of fear; it's one of resolve. She had thought about what she might do if the unimaginable happened. She was mentally and emotionally ready to protect her students because she had made the decision long before the moment came.

Preparedness is not about living in fear. It's about reducing fear through training, awareness, and clarity.

You Are the Constant

In an emergency, everything becomes uncertain—except you. You are the familiar voice, the steady presence, the adult your students know and trust.

That's why this book isn't about turning you into a responder with a radio or badge. It's about recognizing that your leadership—especially in the **first five minutes**—is irreplaceable.

You are not alone. You are part of a team. But **you are also the leader your students will look to first.**

Let's take a closer look at the tools and strategies that will help you be ready—mentally, emotionally, and practically—for whatever comes next.

Chapter 2

Understanding the SHELL Protocols from the Classroom Perspective

In a moment of crisis, there's no time to second-guess. That's why the SHELL acronym is so powerful—it gives schools a shared language and a clear set of actions for five types of emergencies.

SHELL stands for Shelter in Place, Hold in Place, Evacuation, Lockout, and Lockdown. Each protocol represents a specific emergency response designed to help teachers and students know exactly what to do and when to do it.

For teachers, the key isn't memorizing a binder. It's understanding what each protocol means in your room, with your students, right now.

This chapter will walk you through:

1. **What each SHELL action is**

2. **When to use it**

3. **The steps to take**

4. **How to support students based on their age and development**

We'll also share real insights we've seen in action from schools just like yours.

S – Shelter in Place

What it is:
Used when there's an **environmental threat outside**—the safest option is to stay inside and seal the building.

When to use it:

- Gas leak nearby

- Chemical spill or hazardous material incident

- Poor air quality from smoke or fire

- Severe weather approaching

Steps to Take:

- Shut and lock all windows and doors

- Turn off classroom fans or HVAC if possible

- Block air gaps—if available, use painter's tape or plastic sheeting from your emergency kit

- Keep students in the room; do not send anyone into hallways or other areas

- Reverse evacuation for anyone outside

- Maintain calm, continue light activity (reading, drawing, journaling)

- Monitor communications for the all-clear

Personal Approach – Lower School (5–7 years):
We've seen a kindergarten teacher dim the lights, gather her students on the rug, and say:

> *"There's something outside that we don't want to breathe in. So we're having quiet indoor time while the helpers fix it."*
>
> She pulled out a storybook and read in a whisper, creating a calm atmosphere. One student even told her it felt like "camping in the classroom."

Upper Elementary (8–10 years):
You can be a little more direct:

> *"There's a chemical leak in the area. We're staying put until the air is safe. We're completely fine in here."*

Let them draw or write. One fourth-grade teacher gave her class a writing prompt:

> *"What do you like about our classroom?"*
> It kept them focused on the positive and grounded in their environment.

H – Hold in Place

What it is:
Used when movement in the building needs to stop temporarily. Often it's a medical emergency or situation in the hallway.

When to use it:

- Student has a medical emergency in hallway
- Physical altercation needs to be cleared
- Custodial or emergency crew needs the space cleared
- Suspicious smell, spill, or investigation in progress

Steps to Take:

- Keep students in your room—no hallway movement
- Continue instruction as usual
- Lock your door if instructed
- Reassure students the situation is not inside your classroom
- Await the "all clear" to resume normal activities

Personal Approach – Lower School (5–7 years):
One 1st-grade teacher told her students:

> *"Someone outside our room needs help, so we're staying put so the helpers can do their job."*

She gave each table a soft task—Legos, crayons, puzzles—then circled quietly, checking in with each student.

Upper Elementary (8–10 years):
Students this age benefit from straightforward language. Try:

"There's a situation outside the room. We're being respectful by staying in place so others can do their job."

Give them low-key, engaging work. A short journaling exercise or classroom trivia works great here.

E – Evacuation

What it is:
Used when **it's not safe to stay in the building**—you need to move students outside to a designated assembly area.

When to use it:

- Fire alarm or smoke detected

- Gas smell or unknown odor

- Structural integrity issue (e.g., flooding, ceiling damage)

- Bomb threat

Steps to Take:

- Stay calm—your tone will guide your students

- Line up your class in a practiced order (e.g., by classroom number or assigned buddy)

- Bring your attendance list if possible

- Leave immediately using the assigned evacuation route

- Make sure you know a secondary route in case primary route is unavailable

- Take attendance at the assembly area and report any issues

- Remain at location until further instructions

Personal Approach – Lower School (5–7 years):
One pre-K teacher we worked with kept a "grab bag" by the door—roster, stickers, and even a small wind-up toy. She told her students:

> *"We're going on a safety walk. Remember how we practiced? Let's hold hands and stay with our buddy."*
> The toy came out after roll call. It turned anxiety into calm.

Upper Elementary (8–10 years):
These students can manage more responsibility. Use calm but direct language:

> *"There's an issue in the building—we're leaving to stay safe. Line up and stay silent until we get to our spot."*

Assign roles: door opener, attendance checker, runner. Let them feel empowered in the routine.

L – Lockout

What it is:
Used when the **threat is outside the building**—we lock all exterior doors, but teaching continues inside.

When to use it:

- Police activity in the area

- Person of concern near campus

- Nearby disturbance or protest

- Dangerous wild animal outside school grounds

Steps to Take:

- Continue teaching inside the classroom (keep the topics light [e.g. pause exams])

- Do not send anyone outside, including for recess or pickup

- Lock doors (admin typically does this)

- Stay alert for updates

- Keep movement inside the building normal

- Reverse Evacuation for anyone who is outside the building

Personal Approach – Lower School (5–7 years):
We saw a 2nd-grade teacher use it as "Indoor Recess Adventure." She said:

> *"There's something outside we're staying away from, so today's all inside fun."*

She gave students indoor jobs (recess helper, clean-up captain) to keep them feeling safe and in control.

Upper Elementary (8–10 years):
A fifth-grade teacher we worked with told her class:

> *"There's police activity nearby. We're just playing it safe by staying inside."*

She let them keep working but gave occasional updates to maintain trust.

L – Lockdown

What it is:
Used when there's a **direct threat inside or near the school**. This is the most serious of the SHELL protocols.

When to use it:

- Armed intruder

- Violent threat inside the building

- Directed threat to a classroom or staff member

Steps to Take:

- Lock the door, turn off lights, cover windows if possible

- Barricade the door with anything you can

- Move students to your hiding location (low and out of sight)

- Maintain absolute silence

- Silence phones

- Do not open the door for anyone until cleared by law enforcement or admin

- Prepare students for a potentially extended wait

Personal Approach – Lower School (5–7 years):
During one real lockdown drill, a kindergarten teacher whispered to her students:

> *"Let's pretend we're animals in the forest—we need to be as quiet as a bunny."*
> They huddled under a table with a class blanket and counted silent fingers together until it was over. The teacher later said,
> *"They followed my mood more than anything else."*

We recommend keeping candy on standby. Perhaps a bag of lollipops all the same flavor to eliminate fighting.

Upper Elementary (8–10 years):
These students are more aware. Be firm and brief:

> *"This is a lockdown. You know what to do. Follow me and stay silent. We're going to be okay."*

They'll look to you for signals. Use calm hand gestures, reassuring eye contact, and stillness. After the lockdown ends, always take time to decompress—even just five quiet minutes of coloring, journaling, or sitting in a circle can help release tension.

Let us be clear: **you don't need to be perfect** in these moments. You just need to be prepared, calm, and connected to your students. That's what they'll remember—and that's what keeps them safe.

Part II: Responding in Real Time

Chapter 3

The Art of Calm – Communicating Under Pressure

When the alarm sounds, the lights go off, or a lockdown announcement echoes over the PA, your students turn to you.

They don't care about the name of the protocol. They care about **you**—your tone, your face, your words. In those moments, you are their anchor. The calm you project is the calm they absorb.

This chapter is about developing that calm—not just pretending to be composed, but learning how to **communicate effectively and purposefully under stress.**

Why Calm Communication Matters

We've seen it firsthand: the difference between a smooth evacuation and a chaotic one often comes down to the teacher's voice.

Students don't always remember the plan—but they always remember *how it felt*. A calm, steady adult voice gives them the safety and structure they need, even in uncertainty.

How to Speak in Crisis

Here are some practical strategies we've seen work across grade levels:

1. Use Simple, Declarative Language

Avoid vague terms. Instead of:

> *"Okay everyone, um, I think we need to get ready to leave…"*
> Say:
> *"Line up now. We're evacuating. Quiet voices."*

Use short phrases. Clarity builds confidence.

2. Keep Your Tone Low and Even

A raised voice—even if not angry—can signal panic. A quiet, steady tone has the opposite effect. We once heard a teacher use a whisper during a Shelter in Place:

> *"We're all safe right now. We're staying inside and doing our jobs. Let's take out our books."*

That whisper worked better than any drill.

3. Control Your Face and Body

Your facial expression tells a story. We worked with a school where the teacher practiced "neutral face, calm hands" during drills. She never smiled too much (which can feel false), but she never looked afraid. She simply stayed steady.

Try this:

- Keep your body still

- Use slow hand motions

- Avoid pacing or sudden gestures

What to Say – And What Not to Say

☑ Helpful Phrases	✗ Avoid These
"We know what to do."	"I don't know what's going on."
"I'm right here with you."	"This is bad."
"We've practiced this."	"I'm freaking out too."
"You're doing great."	"Calm down!"

Talking to Different Age Groups

Lower School (5–7 years)

Children this age mirror you emotionally. One teacher told us:

> *"They didn't even ask questions—they just watched my face. So I kept it soft."*

What works:

- Whispered directions
- Visual cues (pointing, hand signals)

- Short affirmations:

    "We're doing the safe thing right now."

Avoid:

- Overloading with information
- Letting other students talk over you—this can create confusion

Upper Elementary (8–10 years)

They're more aware—but they still need *you* to model control. Be direct, but don't get pulled into "what if" conversations.

Try:

  "I don't have every detail, but I do know this—we're following the plan, and I've got you."

Let them ask questions *after* the moment passes—not during the heat of it.

If you practice these drills many of their questions can be answered before the real thing.

Grounding Yourself in the Moment

Even the most seasoned teachers feel nerves during an emergency. Here's what you can do:

- Take one slow breath before giving your first direction

- Use grounding phrases *for yourself,* silently:

    "I am calm. I am focused. I know the plan."

- Focus on the one student who needs you the most in that moment—ground your energy in helping them

After the Moment Passes

When the all-clear is given, don't rush right back into instruction. Even a 2–3 minute reset can make a huge difference.

We saw one third-grade teacher who had a post-drill ritual:

"Take a breath. High five a friend. Say one thing you're proud of."

That teacher created emotional closure, not just procedural wrap-up.

Final Thought

Calm isn't about **never being afraid**. It's about staying centered in the face of fear. When students hear your steady voice and see your steady presence, they feel secure—even when they don't fully understand what's happening.

Your calm is more than a tone. It's a tool. And it might be the most important one you have.

Chapter 4

Leading Students When the Alarm Sounds

You hear the tone.

Your heart skips—but your students are watching you.

The truth is, when a fire alarm rings or a lockdown is announced, **students don't look to the front office. They look to you.** And what you do in the next 10 seconds will shape how they respond for the rest of the emergency.

This chapter is about those moments—the instant the emergency starts, and you shift from "teaching" to "leading."

Leadership Is a Behavior, Not a Title

You don't need to be a department chair or veteran teacher to be a leader. In fact, some of the best leadership we've seen has come from new teachers who simply stayed calm, made decisions quickly, and focused on their students.

Leadership in an emergency isn't about authority. It's about **clarity, control, and confidence**—and it starts before you even leave your desk.

What Happens First: Your First Move

When an alarm sounds or an announcement is made, teachers often freeze—not from fear, but from uncertainty. The brain rushes to process:

- *What kind of emergency is this?*

- *What does my protocol say?*

- *What do I do with my students?*

The best way to avoid this freeze is to pre-load your first action.

We suggest mentally rehearsing three key steps for each protocol. For example:

Evacuation:

1. Grab clipboard with roster

2. Line up students by the door

3. Check hallway, then begin moving

Lockdown:

1. Lock door and lights off

2. Direct students to the hiding spot

3. Silence and wait

Knowing those three steps helps you lead decisively.

Your Voice: Set the Tone Immediately

The first 10 seconds set the emotional tone. Speak clearly and without panic:

> *"We're doing a lockdown. You know what to do. Let's move."*
> *"It's an evacuation. Line up—grab nothing—stay quiet."*

No yelling. No rushing. Your calm will carry more authority than volume ever will.

Supporting Students Through the Transition

Students don't always respond the way we expect.

We've seen everything:

- Students who freeze and won't move
- Students who start asking loud, anxious questions
- Students who try to joke or distract to cope with fear

Your job isn't to solve every emotional reaction—but it is to **acknowledge and redirect**.

What works:

- "I see you're nervous. That's okay. Stay with me—we're going together."

- "We're moving now. Talking can wait. Right now we're focusing on being safe."

Sometimes, just making **eye contact** with a scared student gives them the confidence to follow.

Role Assignment: Let Students Help

Older elementary students respond well to having small responsibilities.

Try this:

- **Door opener** (if safe)

- **Buddy checker**

- **Line leader or tail monitor**

- **Emergency kit carrier**

One fifth-grade teacher we worked with said:

> *"I told my students: 'When the alarm sounds, we're a team. Everyone has a role.' That changed everything."*

They practiced rotating roles during drills—and when the real moment came, students moved with purpose.

Accounting for Students

One of your most important leadership duties is making sure every student is present and accounted for—especially after movement (evacuation or lockdown).

Here's what we recommend:

- Keep your **roster or emergency folder by the door** or in a designated "go bag"

- After evacuating, do a **headcount first**, then a name check

- If a student is missing, notify leadership **immediately and quietly**—never leave the group

Pro tip: If you teach younger students, assign them buddies. For special needs students or those with mobility issues, make sure plans are individualized and practiced.

Resetting the Room After the Emergency

Once the emergency ends, your students will still look to you.

We've seen schools jump straight back into instruction after a stressful drill or incident—but your class will respond better if you **take a few minutes to reset**.

Simple options:

- "Take a breath, grab water, then meet me at the rug."

- "Share one word to describe how you're feeling, then we'll move on together."

- 2-minute quiet drawing time

The message you send is:

> *"That was serious, but we're okay—and we're still a community."*

Final Thought: You're the Constant

In any emergency, there's one thing that doesn't change: **you**.

Not the announcement, not the alarm, not the noise or confusion. You. The teacher. The adult in the room who leads by example, even when you're scared too.

Your students may not remember what the alarm sounded like—but they'll remember what *you* sounded like.

They'll remember how they felt when they looked at you.

Part III: Prevention and Awareness

Chapter 5

Recognizing Red Flags – Behavior Before Crisis

Most school emergencies don't start with sirens. They start with **behavior**. Words muttered under a breath. A drawing that feels darker than usual. A student who was once chatty suddenly silent.

In threat assessment, **prevention begins with observation**. And no one is better positioned to notice small changes than teachers.

This chapter will show you how to spot early warning signs, understand the difference between **transient and substantive threats**, and know how to respond—not as an investigator, but as a frontline observer who can activate a school's safety systems.

Why Teachers Matter in Threat Assessment

You are the first layer of defense—not because you're security personnel, but because you're **relationally connected** to students. You notice when something's off.

Threat assessment experts agree: most students who committed acts of targeted school violence **displayed concerning behavior beforehand**, and in nearly every case, **someone knew**—often a peer or teacher.

Your job is not to label a student as dangerous. Your job is to:

- Notice patterns

- Document concerns

- Share what you see—early and clearly

That one conversation you start? It might be the thing that prevents a tragedy.

Know Their Baseline

One of the most effective tools a teacher has is simple: **paying attention to what's normal**.

We call this "learning the baseline." It means you know what a student typically sounds like, how they move, how they engage, and how they handle stress on an average day.

When you know the baseline, it becomes much easier to notice when something is off—whether that's a sudden withdrawal, an uncharacteristic outburst, or subtle shifts in posture, eye contact, or tone.

Threat assessment isn't just about identifying dangerous behavior. It's about recognizing *changes* that may signal a student is in distress or needs support—*before* things escalate.

CSTAG's Core Concept: Transient vs. Substantive Threats

The CSTAG model (Comprehensive School Threat Assessment Guidelines) gives schools a roadmap for managing threats. But here's what matters most for teachers:

Not all threats are the same.

- ◇ **Transient Threats**

    - Are not serious or not intended to be carried out

    - Often made in anger, frustration, humor, or competition

    - Can be resolved with explanation, apology, or mild consequence

Examples:

- "I'm going to kill you in dodgeball!" (playful tone)

- "I hate this class—I could just explode." (venting)

If it's a transient threat, your role is still critical. Document it, report it, and let the team confirm that it's not escalating.

- ◇ **Substantive Threats**

    - Are more serious and indicate potential intent to harm

    - Often involve planning, repetition, or fixation on violence

    - Require protective action and may involve law enforcement

Examples:

- "I've been thinking about bringing something to school."

- "They're all going to pay. Just wait."

- Drawings or writings with repeated violent imagery, names, or specific plans

You don't need to know which type it is. That's what the school team is for. But **reporting it accurately** helps your school take the right next step.

A Note on Language: "Care Team" Over "Threat Assessment Team"

While many schools use the term **Threat Assessment Team**, we prefer the phrase **Care Team**—and we encourage schools to adopt that language where possible.

The goal of this process is not to label, punish, or remove students. It's to **notice when someone is in distress** and activate a supportive, well-coordinated response. The word "care" better reflects the intention: **to intervene early, offer help, and prevent harm.**

No matter what your school calls the team, the core mission is the same: see something, say something, and give the student a path forward—not a dead end.

What to Watch For – Teacher-Specific Red Flags

You see your students in multiple contexts—lessons, transitions, unstructured moments. These are the things we've trained teachers to watch for:

1. Behavioral Shifts

- Sudden withdrawal, silence, or emotional volatility

- Frequent outbursts or intense reactions to small frustrations

- Fixation on a topic—especially death, violence, revenge

2. Written or Creative Work

- Stories, journal entries, or drawings with repeated violent themes

- Assignments mentioning weapons, "getting even," or hopelessness

- Excessive personalization in violent content (naming classmates, teachers)

3. Social Signs

- Isolation from peers

- "Leakage"—hinting at something big coming, or saying "you'll see"

- Glorification of past school shooters or violent figures

4. Statements to You or Peers

- "You'll be sorry."

- "They're all going to regret how they treated me."

- "I don't care what happens anymore."

Always take this seriously—even if the student laughs it off afterward.

What to Do (Even If You're Unsure)

Let's be clear: you don't need to investigate. You need to **describe** what you saw and **pass it along**.

Use this simple formula:

Who, What, When, Where, How

- WHO made the statement or showed the behavior?

- WHAT exactly was said, written, or drawn?

- WHEN and WHERE did it happen?

- HOW did it seem—tone of voice, body language?

Write it down while it's fresh. Don't rely on memory. Stick to **objective facts**, not interpretations.

Then report it. To your administrator, counselor, or designated safety lead.

Remember: **you're not reporting a student—you're reporting a behavior.**

How to Check In With a Student (If It Feels Right)

If the student isn't presenting a direct threat, but something feels off, you may want to initiate a private conversation.

Here are some teacher-tested phrases:

- *"You haven't seemed like yourself lately. Want to talk?"*

- *"That story you wrote—there was a lot going on. What was on your mind when you wrote it?"*

- *"I noticed you've been quieter than usual. I care about how you're doing."*

The goal here isn't to diagnose or confront—it's to let the student know you see them. Then, pass it on.

Real Story: The Creative Writing Assignment

At a school we worked with, a teacher noticed that a normally upbeat 6th grader turned in a series of increasingly violent short stories—always ending in revenge or destruction.

The teacher followed her instincts. She didn't accuse the student, but she submitted the work to the school counselor with a note:

> *"This might be nothing—but I've never seen this side of him before."*

It wasn't "nothing." The student was being harassed online and had stopped telling adults. A threat assessment followed, counseling was initiated, and the student eventually opened up.

The teacher didn't make the decision—but she made the difference.

The NTAC Principle: Someone Almost Always Knows

The U.S. Secret Service's National Threat Assessment Center (NTAC) concluded that **in nearly every school attack**, someone—usually a peer or teacher—had prior knowledge or concern.

They emphasize:

- **Behavioral threat assessment is the best prevention method**

- **Most attackers had shared their intent or distress in advance**

- **Early intervention leads to positive outcomes—not punishment, but support**

Final Thought: You're the Eyes and Ears

Every safety plan in the world relies on what someone notices. And in schools, it's usually a teacher.

You don't need to know all the steps of CSTAG or NTAC. You just need to remember:

- Notice patterns

- Trust your instincts

- Describe what you see

- Share it with the right person

And always, always believe that what you notice—no matter how small—might be the thing that keeps everyone safe.

Chapter 6

De-Escalation in the Classroom

How to Respond, Not React, When Emotions Run High

Not every threat looks like a threat at first. In most schools, the real work of keeping people safe doesn't start with a lockdown—it starts with a moment. A sudden outburst. A slammed desk. A phrase muttered under breath.

The key to preventing escalation is recognizing **emotional overload early** and meeting it with calm, not control. And the person best positioned to do that? You.

You Are the Regulator

When a student escalates—whether it's frustration, embarrassment, fear, or anger—someone in the room has to hold the line. Not with volume or power, but with **regulated behavior**. That someone is you.

> *"If I lose control, the room will too. But if I stay calm, I give them a way back."*
> That's what a 6th grade teacher told us after de-escalating a shouting match between two students during group work.

Early Warning Signs of Escalation

Escalation doesn't happen out of nowhere. It builds. When you learn to spot it early, you can intervene early—before things blow up.

Watch for:

- Change in breathing (faster, more shallow)

- Repetitive speech or pacing

- Clenched fists, tensed shoulders, "locked" jaw

- Eyes darting, standing abruptly, knocking over materials

- "Snapping" at small requests (e.g., "Why do I have to do this?!")

Pro tip: Don't wait until a student *blows up*. De-escalation is most effective when you intervene at the *first signs of emotional distress*.

The Power of Active Listening

When a student is escalating, one of the most powerful things you can do is **shut up and listen**.

We don't say that flippantly. In the heat of the moment, our instinct is to **talk the student down**—but often, what they need is someone who will just *hear them* without judgment or correction.

Active listening means:

- Facing the student with open body language

- Making eye contact (unless that escalates them—know your students)

- Using **minimal encouragers** like "Okay," "I hear you," "Go on"

- Reflecting feelings:

    "It sounds like you felt embarrassed when that happened."

- Asking clarifying questions—not interrogation, but curiosity:

    "What happened right before that?"
    "What did you need in that moment?"

When a student feels heard, they don't need to shout to prove their point. Often, they just need **someone safe enough to unload on.**

Say This, Not That – Language Swaps That Help

✗ Don't Say This…	✓ Try This Instead…
"Calm down!"	"Take a breath with me."
"Because I said so."	"Here's why this matters."

"What's wrong with you?"	"Help me understand what's going on."
"Stop acting like that."	"Let's talk about what's making this hard."
"Go sit down!"	"Let's figure out a better spot for you right now."

These small shifts in language remove the **power struggle** and replace it with **guided support**.

Give Them a Way Back

Students often escalate when they feel:

- Cornered

- Disrespected

- Hopeless or powerless

- Like they're being watched or shamed

We've seen teachers *lower the heat* by offering students a "graceful exit"—a way to reset without feeling punished.

> *"Do you want to step out for a minute and come back when you're ready?"*
> *"Would it help to move to the back table for now?"*
> *"You can use your break card if you need space."*

This **doesn't mean letting them off the hook**—it means giving them dignity while they regroup.

What De-Escalation Isn't

Let's be clear. De-escalation does **not** mean:

- Ignoring bad behavior
- Allowing harm to others
- Letting students run the room
- Avoiding accountability

De-escalation is **not the absence of consequences**—it's the *presence of emotional control* so that consequences can be delivered **effectively, not reactively**.

Real Story: The Math Meltdown

A teacher we work with shared this:

> "My 5th grader couldn't get a long division problem. He crumpled his paper, threw his pencil, and shouted, 'This is so stupid!' Everyone turned to look."

Her first instinct was to correct him in front of the class. Instead, she took a breath and said:

> *"Take a minute. You're frustrated—that's okay. Let's figure it out when you're ready."*

She let him step into the hallway, then followed. Five minutes later, they were working through the problem together, and he was back with the group by the next activity.

> *"That moment could've gone a very different way,"* she said. *"I just didn't want to add more fuel."*

De-Escalation Tools That Work

Physical Tools:

- Break cards
- Calming corner
- Noise-canceling headphones
- Soft sensory items (fidgets, putty)
- Visual breathing guides

Verbal Tools:

- "You're safe."
- "I hear you."
- "You're not in trouble—I just want to help."

- "We'll work through this. Right now let's slow down."

Behavioral Tools:

- Controlled silence
- Slow movement
- Avoid ultimatums
- Physical redirection (only when trained)
- Calling for assistance *before* things spiral

Final Thought: Calm Is Contagious

The classroom is a mirror. If your voice gets sharper, your students will match it. If your posture gets defensive, they'll notice. But if you keep your **breath steady, your voice calm, your words intentional**, they will almost always follow your lead.

You're not just managing a behavior—you're modeling a way of responding to difficulty.

In that moment, **you're not just a teacher. You're the safe adult.** And that is powerful.

Chapter 7

When Police Arrive

What to Expect—and How to Support Your Students—When Law Enforcement Responds to a School Emergency

In an emergency, your focus is your classroom: protecting, calming, and leading your students.

But when law enforcement arrives, the situation enters a new phase—**one where roles shift**, tension may rise, and decisions happen fast. For teachers, that moment can feel disorienting.

This chapter will walk you through what to expect, what to do, and how to support your students when the police take over.

What You Need to Know About Police Response

When police respond to a potential threat in a school, their first priority is not information gathering or medical aid—it's to **stop the threat.**

They are trained to:

- Move quickly and decisively

- Ignore injured parties (initially)

- Treat everyone as a potential threat until cleared

This can feel **cold, confusing, even frightening**—especially for students and teachers who've just been hiding or sheltering.

Understanding their objectives helps you stay grounded and keep your students calm.

Expect This Behavior from Officers:

- They may have **weapons drawn**

- They may **not explain what's happening**

- They may **shout commands** in a loud, direct voice

- They may **not identify themselves immediately**

- They are often **hyper-focused** on threat cues (movement, hands, non-compliance)

This is standard and intentional. It does *not* mean something is wrong—it means they're working to neutralize danger as efficiently as possible.

What You Should Do When Police Enter Your Room

☑ **DO:**

- Keep your **hands visible** at all times

- Remain calm, still, and silent unless addressed

- **Follow commands** immediately—no matter how abrupt they sound

- Identify yourself **only when asked**

- Wait for direction before moving students

✗ DON'T:

- Shout, wave, or run toward officers

- Reach into bags, drawers, or desks without being told

- Try to explain what happened in that moment—they're not gathering statements yet

- Touch officers or try to stop them

One officer told us:

> "If I point my weapon at a classroom door, and it opens from the inside without command, my job is to react—not assume. That's why containment is so critical."

How to Support Students During Police Entry

For many students—especially young children—police presence can cause intense anxiety. It's not unusual for a child to cry, freeze, or panic when they see armed responders.

Your role:

- Use a **low, steady voice**: "You're safe. The police are here to help. Stay quiet. Stay still."

- Keep students in place until directed to move

- Maintain physical closeness if appropriate (especially with younger students)

- Reassure them silently with gestures—hand on shoulder, eye contact, head nod

If possible, **be the still point in the room**. Even if your heart is racing, your calmness becomes their guide.

Once Cleared: Be Ready to Move

After officers determine your room is safe, they may direct you to:

- Line up students and exit

- Keep hands raised while exiting

- Move to a reunification or staging area

Prepare your students with short, clear directions:

> *"We're going to walk out. Keep your hands up. Stay in line. No talking."*

Bring your roster or emergency folder if you can—but **don't go back for it**. Student safety comes first.

Real-World Insight: Why This Feels So Different

Teachers are used to *explaining*, *comforting*, and *leading with empathy*.

But police operations are structured for speed, not sensitivity. That's not a flaw—it's the reality of neutralizing a threat.

Knowing that ahead of time makes the moment feel less jarring—and helps you interpret actions not as aggression, but as **strategic urgency**.

Final Thought: Stay Calm, Stay Visible, Stay Focused

When police arrive, your job shifts slightly: From leading the response… to **supporting the transition.**

Your calm behavior helps students stay regulated. Your quick compliance keeps everyone safer. And your awareness of what's coming next makes a high-intensity moment just a little easier to manage.

In the next chapter, we'll talk about what happens **after** the responders leave—and how you help your students (and yourself) recover.

Part IV: Resilience and Recovery

Chapter 8

After the Emergency – Recovery Starts With You

Helping Students—and Yourself—Reset, Reflect, and Reconnect

The lockdown ends. The responders leave. The PA system goes silent.

And suddenly, it's just you and your students again. A room full of people trying to go back to "normal" when things don't quite feel normal yet.

This chapter is about what comes *next*—the often-overlooked emotional reset that turns fear into safety, and adrenaline into calm.

Whether it was a drill, a threat, or a real incident, **your presence and leadership in the aftermath** are just as important as what you did during the emergency itself.

Reunification – The Final Step in the Emergency Journey

Once the threat has passed and first responders have cleared the scene, schools enter a final—but incredibly sensitive—phase: **reunification.** This is when students are released to their caregivers, usually in a controlled location and under tight supervision.

For teachers, reunification can feel chaotic. Emotions are high, logistics are complex, and students look to you for both information and reassurance.

What Teachers Should Know

- **You may be asked to escort students to a reunification site** (often a gym, church, or off-campus location)

- **You might assist in verifying IDs or checking off student rosters**

- **You may need to comfort students** who are scared, crying, or waiting longer than expected to see their family

"One of the hardest parts was not being able to answer when they'd see their parents. I just kept saying, 'We're here together. That's what matters right now.'"
– 4th Grade Teacher, New Jersey

Your Checklist at a Reunification Site

- Bring your class roster or emergency folder

- Keep students grouped together

- Stay in communication with admin or safety lead

- Document each student's release time and who picked them up

- Never release a student without formal clearance from the reunification team

What to Say to Students

> *"Your grown-up is coming. It may take a little while, but they know where we are."*
>
> *"We're staying right here until it's your turn—I'll be with you the whole time."*

Reunification is as much about **emotional closure** as it is logistics. Your steady presence is what makes that possible.

The Brain Needs to Come Down

Emergencies activate the nervous system—heart racing, muscles tense, mind on high alert. Even drills can trigger this response.

You may see:

- Students visibly shaken or fidgety
- Students hyper-silly or emotionally "off"
- Quiet students suddenly needing reassurance
- Avoidance behaviors (e.g., "I need to go to the nurse")

The goal isn't to pretend nothing happened. The goal is to **regulate and reconnect.**

Step 1: Reset the Room

Start with grounding. Even 3–5 minutes of quiet recovery helps the class center themselves.

Ideas that work:

- "Take a breath and draw how you're feeling right now."

- Calm music while students color or write in journals

- Share one word about how you feel—no pressure to explain

- Water break, breathing exercise, or short walk (if allowed)

A second-grade teacher we worked with always said:

> *"Let's get our hearts and our brains back in the same place."*

It became a ritual after every drill.

Step 2: Briefly Talk About It—If It's Appropriate

Some classes will need a moment to debrief. Some won't. Use your judgment.

For younger students:

- "That was a serious drill. We stayed safe and followed directions. I'm proud of you."

- "Do you have any questions about what we just did?"

- "What helped you feel calm during that?"

For older students:

- Ask: "What went well? What was hard?"
- Give space for reflection, but don't force it
- Validate all responses—even silence

Avoid:

- Downplaying the experience ("It was nothing")
- Overexplaining with fear-based language
- Forcing students to talk if they're not ready

Step 3: Watch for Individual Student Needs

Some students may experience delayed reactions. Others may internalize their anxiety and not speak up unless prompted one-on-one.

Look for:

- Sudden withdrawal or silence
- Tearfulness or difficulty focusing
- Repeated questions about the emergency

- Physical complaints (headache, stomachache)

Reach out gently. Loop in school counselors as needed. Sometimes the simple act of saying,

> *"Hey, I noticed you've been quiet—want to talk later?"*
> makes all the difference.

Step 4: Check In With Yourself

You experienced the same emergency your students did—and you carried the emotional weight of 20+ other people at the same time.

You might feel:

- Exhausted

- Shaky

- Emotionally disconnected

- Guilty (e.g., "Could I have done more?")

All of that is normal. But it doesn't mean you have to carry it alone.

Try this:

- Step into the hallway or teacher lounge for a quiet moment

- Debrief with a trusted colleague

- Write a quick reflection:

> *"What worked?"*
> *"What felt hard?"*
> *"What do I need next time?"*

If your school offers staff wellness or counseling, **use it.** Strong teachers aren't the ones who never feel stress—they're the ones who know when to ask for support.

Real Story: The Five-Minute Reset

After a particularly intense lockdown drill, a third-grade teacher gathered her class in a circle. She asked:

> *"Raise your hand if your body still feels a little jumpy."*

Almost every hand went up.

She said:

> *"Me too. Let's get those feelings out with some deep breaths and some drawing. Then we'll move on when we're ready."*

They spent five quiet minutes in reflection—and the class returned to the lesson feeling connected and safe again.

Sometimes, the most powerful recovery tool is just acknowledging what everyone is already feeling.

Final Thought: You're Still Leading—Even After

Recovery isn't about fixing everything. It's about making space—for breath, for safety, and for emotional closure.

You don't need to have perfect words. You don't need to lead a therapy session. You just need to **be there**, grounded, calm, and human.

That's the kind of leadership students remember. And it's the kind that builds resilience for the next challenge—whatever it may be.

Chapter 9

Facing the Fear – Changing the Culture Starts with Us

Why Preparedness Begins with Acknowledging the Stories We Carry

We talk a lot about readiness—what to do, how to lead, when to respond. But we don't talk enough about what's **really** in the way of school preparedness.

It's not just lack of training.
It's not just unclear policy.
It's fear. Real, human fear.

And not always from personal experience. Often, it's from something more invisible: the **accumulation of other people's trauma.**

The Stories That Live in Our Heads

Every time there's a school shooting, teachers take in another story:

- A teacher who died shielding students

- A substitute who didn't know the lockdown protocol

- A custodian who ran toward the sound of gunfire

- A classroom where no one made it out

These stories don't fade. They lodge in our minds and stay there, quietly shaping how we think about our jobs, our students, our schools—and ourselves.

And the truth is, many teachers have become so emotionally saturated by these stories that they begin to **disengage** from preparedness altogether.

Not because they don't care.
Because they care too much—and it hurts.

What Is Vicarious and Secondary Trauma?

> **Vicarious trauma** is what happens when hearing about others' trauma becomes traumatic in itself.
> **Secondary trauma** is what happens when supporting or imagining others in crisis changes the way we experience stress, safety, or our role in the world.

You don't have to witness violence firsthand to be changed by it. You just have to carry the stories.

And teachers carry a lot.

Why Kaitlyn Roig's Story Inspires—And Hurts

When we opened this book, we told the story of Kaitlyn Roig, the first-grade teacher at Sandy Hook who saved her students' lives by hiding them in a bathroom. We told it because her actions reflect the kind of leadership this manual was built to support—calm, protective, instinctive.

But there's another reason we bring her up again.

We've met teachers who can't hear her story without crying. We've seen educators silently leave the room when we mention Sandy Hook. Not because they don't care—but because they've already imagined themselves in that same moment. A locked door. A classroom full of kids. A split-second decision.

> That's vicarious trauma.
> That's what it means to carry the emotional residue of someone else's crisis.

And it's real.

The more these stories accumulate—Uvalde, Parkland, Sandy Hook—the harder it becomes for teachers to engage. Not because they're unwilling, but because the fear is already living inside them. The thought of preparing for it makes the fear louder, not smaller.

Why Some Teachers Avoid the Conversation

In our work, we've seen it over and over:

- Teachers who get visibly upset during lockdown drills

- Teachers who disengage during safety PDs

- Teachers who joke about protocols—not because they're flippant, but because it's their way of deflecting fear

They've absorbed too much to face the topic directly. And so they pull back. They say things like:

"If it happens, it happens."
"There's nothing we can really do."
"I just try not to think about it."

We understand those reactions. But the danger is, **disengagement becomes policy.** What starts as emotional self-protection becomes a school-wide culture of avoidance.

And that leaves everyone more vulnerable.

How We Change the Culture: Start with the Fear

We can't build a strong culture of preparedness if we don't **face what's standing in the way.** That means creating schools where:

- Teachers are allowed to say, "This terrifies me."

- Staff are supported when they carry the emotional weight of these stories

- PD sessions and drills acknowledge—not dismiss—the psychological toll

- Administrators understand that **emotional readiness is part of physical readiness**

Culture shifts when we stop pretending fear doesn't exist—and start naming it, holding space for it, and helping each other move through it.

Real Story: "I Couldn't Watch the Video"

At one of our situational awareness trainings, we shared a short clip from Kaitlyn Roig's interview with Diane Sawyer. One teacher left the room before it started. After the session, she told us:

> *"I couldn't do it. Not because I didn't care. Because I've already imagined that moment in my classroom a hundred times. I don't need a video to feel it."*

That teacher wasn't avoiding responsibility. She was carrying trauma.

What she needed wasn't more footage. She needed **a safe conversation**, tools she could actually use, and permission to feel what she was already feeling.

We gave her all three. She's now a team lead for her school's emergency committee.

What Schools Can Do

To truly build a culture of preparedness, schools must:

- Train mental health staff to recognize teacher trauma

- Offer debrief time—not just after real events, but after drills

- Build in structured reflection and recovery

- Normalize staff wellness conversations:

> *"This is hard. You're not weak. You're impacted. And you're not alone."*

We also recommend offering **optional emotional processing groups** after high-intensity drills or incidents, similar to the model used in crisis response teams: 30–60 minute, facilitated, voluntary sessions.

What You Can Do as a Teacher

If this chapter feels personal, you're not alone. We've felt it too.

Here are small, powerful ways you can lead a cultural shift in your school:

- **Talk about it.** Share how these conversations affect you—privately, with colleagues, or during team meetings.

- **Ask for better support.** It's okay to say: "We need more than a drill—we need space to talk about how this feels."

- **Reflect after drills.** Write, breathe, decompress. Let it land.

- **Support others.** If you notice a colleague withdrawing during a drill or PD, check in afterward. No judgment. Just connection.

Final Thought: Courage Is Facing It Anyway

You are not weak because this work affects you.
You are not dramatic because your heart races when the door slams during a drill.
You are not less of a teacher because you cry during a video of another school's tragedy.

You are human.
You are brave.
And when you keep showing up anyway—when you prepare, when you lead, when you steady your voice and guide your students through—it's not just safety.

It's courage.

The real culture shift begins **when we stop trying to be unshakable—and start standing strong, together.**

Sources and Acknowledgements

While the tone, structure, and instructional approach of this manual are original, several frameworks and public resources have significantly influenced its content. We believe in giving credit where it's due, and in acknowledging the foundational work of those who have helped shape the national conversation around school safety and preparedness.

- **S.H.E.L.L. Protocol** – Developed by the **New York State Education Department (NYSED)**, the S.H.E.L.L. framework serves as the foundational emergency response structure used across New York schools. This manual adapts that framework to speak directly to classroom teachers in a practical, human-centered way.
- **CSTAG (Comprehensive School Threat Assessment Guidelines)** – Created by **Dr. Dewey Cornell**, CSTAG provides a research-backed model for identifying and responding to student threats. The concepts presented here are drawn from that work and are applied specifically from a teacher's perspective.
- **U.S. Secret Service – National Threat Assessment Center (NTAC)** – Their extensive research on school violence prevention and pre-incident behaviors helped shape our understanding of early-warning signs and the importance of behavioral threat assessment.
- **CISA (Cybersecurity and Infrastructure Security Agency)** – Their resources on situational awareness and de-escalation techniques have informed some of the language and recommendations used in this manual.
- **Kaitlyn Roig-DeBellis** – The heroic actions of Kaitlyn Roig during the Sandy Hook Elementary School tragedy, and her subsequent interview with **Diane Sawyer**

(ABC/CBS), provided the emotional and conceptual foundation for Chapter 1.

We are deeply grateful for the public availability of these resources and for the work of professionals in law enforcement, education, and mental health who continue to contribute to the safety of our schools.

About the Authors

Kenneth Lacey

Ken Lacey is a Captain with the Yonkers Police Department in NY, currently serving as the Commanding Officer of the Crime Control Strategies Division. He is also the co-owner of First 5 Consulting Group, a firm specializing in school safety and emergency preparedness.

Ken holds a B.S. in Human Services with a concentration in Neurodiversity and specializes in emergency operations, threat assessment, active shooter response, and law enforcement de-escalation. Outside of work, he is a husband to his wife, Sara, and father to three children, Amie, Liam, and Luke.

David Fraszka

David Fraszka, MPS, AEM, is the co-owner of First 5 Consulting Group and a Detective Lieutenant serving as the Commanding Officer of the Intelligence Unit for the Yonkers Police Department. He leads threat assessment investigations, public safety outreach, and school safety programs.

He holds a Master of Professional Studies in Homeland Security from Penn State and a professional certification as an Associate Emergency Manager through the IAEM. David also serves as the Public Health Emergency Preparedness Coordinator for the Greenwich Department of Health. He lives in Westchester, NY with his wife, Brooke, and two sons, Nico and Dean.

Made in the USA
Middletown, DE
22 November 2025